With love to our little angel, Zach
~ Mimi

THE WISE ANIMAL HANDBOOK

Kate B. Jerome

ARCADIA KIDS

Attempt
new
skills
from
time
to
time.

Just **try** to think them **through.**

And if you **find** you're left **behind**....

...then change your point of view.

Try
not
to
think
of just
yourself.

Invent new ways to share.

Stay close to friends whom you can trust.

But always be aware.

Avoid
the
tattle
in the
tale.

Insist that **truth** is **best.**

Embrace with pride the strengths you have.

Demand
to be
impressed.

Enjoy the peace that nature brings.

Ignore what's just for show.

Join forces when the road gets rough.

Admit
when you
don't know.

Remember **family** is the **best.**

Despite the ups and downs.

Don't **hide** from things that you must **face.**

Make
joyful
laughing
sounds.

Eat **healthy** food to **grow** up **strong.**

Be **patient** with your **friends.**

Try not to take a stubborn stand.

Be **quick** to make amends.

Excuse yourself when manners slip.

Be **helpful** every **day.**

Keep **trying**
even when it's **hard.**

But don't forget to play!

And
sing

...and dance each day!

Written by Kate B. Jerome
Design and Production: Lumina Datamatics, Inc.
Coloring Illustrations: Tom Pounders
Research: Eric Nyquist

Cover Images: See back cover

Interior Images: 002 Anetapics/Shutterstock.com; 003 George Green/Shutterstock.com; 004 Sergey Uryadnikov/Shutterstock.com; 005 Gnomeandi/Shutterstock.com; 006 Bruce MacQueen/Shutterstock.com; 007 Henk Bentlage/Shutterstock.com; 008 M.M./Shutterstock.com; 009 Mikael Damkier/Shutterstock.com; 010 Brendan van Son/Shutterstock.com; 011 Michael Pettigrew/Shutterstock.com; 012 StevenRussellSmithPhotos/Shutterstock.com; 013 Pakhnyushchy/Shutterstock.com; 014 Patjo/Shutterstock.com; 015 Quinn Martin/Shutterstock.com; 016 Lincoln Rogers/Shutterstock.com; 017 Dirk Ercken/Shutterstock.com; 018 Karel Gallas/Shutterstock.com; 019 Orangecrush/Shutterstock.com; 020 Guenter-foto/Shutterstock.com; 021 Janecat/Shutterstock.com; 022 Shironina/Shutterstock.com; 023 Annette Shaff/Shutterstock.com; 024 Vitaly Titov/Shutterstock.com; 025 Rohappy/Shutterstock.com; 026 MattiaATH/Shutterstock.com; 027 Otsphoto/Shutterstock.com; 028 FikMik/Shutterstock.com; 029 Four Oaks/Shutterstock.com; 030 Ekaterina Kolomeets/Shutterstock.com; 031 Hugh Lansdown/Shutterstock.com.

Published by Arcadia Kids, a division of Arcadia Publishing and
The History Press, Charleston, SC

For all general information contact Arcadia Publishing at:
Telephone: 843-853-2070
Email: sales@arcadiapublishing.com

For Customer Service and Orders:
Toll Free: 1-888-313-2665
Visit us on the Internet at www.arcadiapublishing.com

Library of Congress Cataloging-in-Publication data is on file with the publisher.

Printed in China

Florida State **Butterfly**

Zebra Longwing

Read Together

The zebra longwing butterfly was named the state butterfly of Florida in 1996.

Florida State Bird

Mockingbird

Read Together

The mockingbird was named the state bird of Florida in 1927. One of the reasons it was chosen as the state bird was for the beautiful songs it sings.

Florida State Animal

Florida Panther

Read Together

The Florida panther became the state animal in 1982 when students from all over the state voted for it.

Florida State Marine Mammal
Manatee

Read Together

The manatee was named the state marine mammal in 1975. These slow-moving "sea cows" love the warm waters of Florida.